CHICAGO PUBLIC LIBRARY
BEVERLY BRANCH
1962 W. 95th STREET
CHICAGO, IL   60643

JUV/
F
3442
.P776
R36
2004
BEVERL

Chicago Public Library

Francisco Pizarro : the exploration of P

W9-BBC-761

10-05

DISCARD

CHICAGO PUBLIC LIBRARY
BEVERLY BRANCH
1962 W. 95th STREET
CHICAGO, IL   60643

The Library of Explorers and Exploration

FRANCISCO PIZARRO

The Exploration of Peru and the Conquest of the Inca

Fred Ramen

the rosen publishing group's
rosen
central

Published in 2004 by The Rosen Publishing Group, Inc.
29 East 21st Street, New York, NY 10010

Copyright © 2004 by The Rosen Publishing Group, Inc.

First Edition

All rights reserved. No part of this book may be reproduced in any form without permission in writing from the publisher, except by a reviewer.

Library of Congress Cataloging-in-Publication Data

Ramen, Fred.
Francisco Pizarro : the exploration of Peru and the Conquest of the Inca / Fred Ramen.— 1st ed.
    p. cm. — (The library of explorers and exploration)
Includes bibliographical references and index.
ISBN 0-8239-3618-X (library binding)
1. Pizarro, Francisco, ca. 1475–1541—Juvenile literature.
2. Peru—History—Conquest, 1522–1548—Juvenile literature.
3. South America—Discovery and exploration—Spanish—Juvenile literature. 4. Incas—Juvenile literature. 5. Explorers—Peru—Biography—Juvenile literature. 6. Explorers—Spain—Biography—Juvenile literature.
I. Title. II. Series.
F3442.P776 R36 2003
985'.02—dc21

                                                    2002004901

Manufactured in the United States of America

CHICAGO PUBLIC LIBRARY
BEVERLY BRANCH
1962 W. 95th STREET
CHICAGO, IL   60643

CONTENTS

FRANCISCO PIZARRO
CONQUEROR OF PERU

Francisco Pizarro, Spanish explorer and conqueror of the Inca Empire, founded the city of Lima, the capital of Peru. He was assassinated in 1541.

INTRODUCTION

POWER AND CONQUEST

By 1527, Francisco Pizarro's expedition to the Americas had already been at sea for several months. Under the guidance of navigator Bartolomé Ruiz, the group had become the first Europeans to sail north to south over the equator in the Pacific Ocean. But Ruiz had turned east, sailing closer to the coast of South America. He was searching for news of a legendary empire of gold said to be somewhere in the region.

One day he sighted a strange craft. It was a large raft made of logs of balsa wood lashed together. At the back of the raft was a thatched hut to shelter passengers. But what most impressed him was the large sail hoisted over the raft; it was the first time that he had seen inhabitants of the New World use a sail.

Ruiz approached the raft carefully. Several of the men on board the strange vessel jumped into the ocean at the sight of the Spanish ship. However, several remained, including a young man the Spanish would later name Filipillo ("Little Phillip") who would become their first translator. Using sign language, Ruiz eagerly questioned the men on the raft. Where were they from? Were there any cities nearby? Above all, did they have any gold?

The native people told them that they were traders from the coast who were sailing to a large city called Tumbes. This was just one city in a mighty empire that had conquered the entire world. And there was more gold in that raft than there was wood.

The people in the expedition had become the first Europeans to encounter subjects of the Inca Empire. Within ten years, that empire—the mightiest in the history of South America and perhaps even the entire New World—would be conquered by the man who had organized the expedition Ruiz was sailing with: Francisco Pizarro.

Pizarro, like his distant cousin Hernán Cortés, who conquered the Aztec Empire in 1521, was also a conquistador. A conquistador was a Spanish soldier trained to "discover" new lands in the name of Spain, convert its native people to Christianity thereby saving their souls, and gain territory and profits in the process. His character, described as ruthless, unyielding, and even cruel, is forever linked with his legacy: Francisco Pizarro eliminated the empire of the Inca without compromise, died for his cause, and changed Spain—as well as the history of the world—forever.

1

THE FIGHTING EMPIRE

The messengers, who were much alarmed and frightened as by something that they had never dreamed of, told the Inca how some strange people never seen before who preached new doctrines and laws had landed on the beach . . . these men were so bold that they did not fear dangerous things; they were stuffed into their clothes, which covered them head to foot; they were white and had beards and a ferocious appearance . . . and when [the Inca] asked from what part of the world they had come, he was told that the messengers only knew that the strangers traveled across the sea in large wooden houses.
—Father Bernabe Cobo, *History of the Inca Empire*

After Columbus's arrival in the Caribbean in 1492, Spain had rapidly built a huge empire in the Americas, one that had brought excessive amounts of gold and silver to King Ferdinand and Queen Isabella, the Spanish monarchs. This was partly the result of good luck—fate that the king and queen had believed Columbus's claim that the earth was smaller than other explorers and cartographers (mapmakers) believed. Columbus thought the shortest route to the islands, and the riches, of the Indies could be found by sailing west.

Los altos Reyes don fernãdo y doña
ysabel y la   Real ifãta
doña   Juana

Columbus believed that the Caribbean Islands were actually bordering Asia, Europe's source of rich spices and silks. But Columbus had not landed near Asia; he had "discovered" an entirely new continent, which was named America in 1507 after another Italian explorer, Amerigo Vespucci. America held riches of its own: wealth that instigated the beginning of the world's Spanish Empire, which in many ways was destined to develop.

The Reconquest

During the eighth century, Spain had been overrun by invaders from North Africa, whom the Spanish called the Moors. Unlike the Spanish, who were Christians, the Moors were Muslims, followers of the religion of Islam. For nearly seven centuries, sections of Spain were under Muslim control. However, the Spanish almost immediately began to resist their conquerors. A series of bloody conflicts raged throughout Spain for centuries. The Spanish called this the *Reconquista*, or Reconquest, and it lasted from AD 711 to 1492. The battles of the Reconquista resulted in many

This is a 1482 illustration of Spanish rulers Ferdinand of Aragon and Isabella of Castile with their daughter Joan. Ferdinand and Isabella's marriage consolidated Spain, but the two kingdoms were still limited to the personal union between the two monarchs. Their combined vision helped Spain build itself as a strong power in Europe and a colonial empire in the Americas.

La Coruña

GALICIA

Santiago

Lugo

ASTURIAS

Oviedo

Leon

O L

Burgos

Pontavedra

Orense

Palencia

C A S T

R. Minho

Valladolid

R. Duer

Oporto

R. Douro

Zamora

Segovia

Salamanca

Avila

MADRID

R. Tagus

L E O

R.   A Tagus

Tole

Caceres

C A S

LISBON

Badajoz

R. Guadiana

Ciudad Real

La Ma

P O R T U G A L

ESTREMADURA

Cordova

R. Guadal

Jaen

ANDALUS

Huelva

Seville

R. Jenil

Granad

S. Vincent

G

C.

R. Gua

C. Trafalgar

Gibraltar

Spain was divided into smaller provinces during Pizarro's lifetime.
Some of these former provinces, such as Aragon, Castile, Andalusia,
Catalonia, and Valencia, can be seen in this historical map.

S. Sebastian

BASQUE
PROVs

FRANCE

Pamplona

NAVARRA

ANDORRA

Andorra

C. Cra

ogrono

R. Ebro

Huesca

Gerona

Soria

ILE

Saragossa

Lerida

R. Segre

CATALONIA

Barcelona

Guadalajara

Tagus

Teruel

R. Ebro

Tarragona

EW

Cuenca

Castellon

ILE

VALENCIA

Valencia

Majorca

Palma

Albacete

R. Jucar

Iviza

cha

MURCIA

C. S. Martin

Formentera

R. Segura

Alicante

Murcia

C. Palos

Cartagena

Almeria

C. Gata

FORMER PROVINCES
OF
SPAIN

terrible acts. Gradually, the Spanish gained the upper hand, finally capturing Granada, the last outpost of the Moors, in 1492, the same year that Columbus set sail for the Indies.

A large and professional army, well-funded by a centralized government, had made the Spanish the fiercest warriors in Europe. Spanish boys learned to fight from a very young age and had many opportunities to use their training. Spain had also entered into conflicts with other European countries, especially France, against whom they had been struggling for many years in Italy. Into this violent world of struggle and conquest was born Francisco Pizarro.

Like many of the conquistadors—a Spanish word meaning "conqueror," a soldier who voyaged to the New World to capture gold and land from the natives—Pizarro was born in Extremadura, in southwestern Spain. The name of the region comes from the Latin words *extrema et dura*, meaning "remote and hard." It is a hot, dusty region during the summer, as well as an area of the world that produces a freezing winter season. Its inhabitants have always been poor but hardy, and the men were considered tough, talented fighters who never forgot an insult. Pizarro's distant cousin Hernán Cortés, the conqueror of Mexico, was from this region as well, as were many of the men who fought under both conquistadors.

A Spanish conquistador rides on horseback through New Spain (Mexico).
Spain held on to its territories in the New World through the military
skills of such conquistadors. A caption below this illustration reads:
"Determined to hold the land against all . . ."

A Soldier's Son

Little is known of Pizarro's early life. Even his birth date is not known with any accuracy; most historians believe it to be around 1475, but it may have been as early as 1470 or as late as 1478. He came from an undistinguished family of soldiers and, although his father was a gentleman, Francisco, an illegitimate child, did not inherit his title. In those days, it was very difficult to change your social status in Spain; the only methods to gain a noble title were either to marry into a noble family or become a great warrior who would be rewarded by the king.

As mentioned before, Pizarro was an illegitimate son, meaning that his father had not married his mother. This normally meant that he was not eligible to inherit his father's property. This was common in Spain at the time since many children were illegitimate. (It was also possible to "legitimize," or make an illegitimate child a legal heir, by appealing to the king. This was common, and Pizarro himself would later do it for his own children.) There are many legends about his early childhood. Some say that he was abandoned by his mother on a church doorstep. Another legend has him actually living with pigs and being given milk by a mother pig, but this is almost certainly not true. He does seem to have lived with his mother's family and been a pig-herder—a respectable job for a commoner—during his youth. Pizarro never received much of an education; to the end of his life he was unable to read or write.

His father, Gonzalo Pizarro, known as "The Tall" and "The One-Eyed," was an army officer who had fought against the Moors; he was never close to Francisco, his first son, and never made him legitimate. Francisco was not his only illegitimate son. Gonzalo left him two half brothers by two women: Gonzalo and Juan Pizarro. The Pizarro brothers—including Hernando—were close, and each was an important figure in the conquest of Peru.

Francisco followed in his father's footsteps and became a soldier, probably in the late 1490s. This was during the exciting period when the first colonies in the New World were being founded and the war against France was being fought in Italy. Pizarro most likely went to Italy in the 1500s and learned much that would help him fight the Inca.

Spain's Master Warriors

At this time, the Spanish were the terror of the battlefields of Europe. Their infantrymen, called *tercios* in Spanish, were masters of fighting together in complicated but deadly maneuvers. Their cavalry, consisting of armored men on horseback who fought with swords or with fourteen-foot lances, were probably the best horsemen in Europe. Like all European armies, the Spanish also used crossbows—heavy bows mounted on wooden stocks. Crossbows could fire a short arrow known as a bolt with such force that it could penetrate steel armor at a distance of several hundred yards. They also used primitive guns called harquebuses. These guns were fired by lowering a piece of burning wick or fuse into a barrel, which, when the trigger was pulled, made contact and fired. Complicated, unreliable, and difficult to reload—the bullet could only be rammed down the barrel with a stick—they were still very deadly and took less training and strength than either regular bows or crossbows. All of these advances helped small numbers of Spanish soldiers defeat huge numbers of Native

An angel holds a harquebus in this seventeenth-century illustration. One of the results of the Spanish conquest of the New World was a unique school of art that flourished for three centuries in the Spanish colonies. This example of an angel in military dress is common in Bolivia's colonial period in the Lake Titicaca region.

Americans. Still, it was not only their mastery of fighting techniques that made the Spanish such great warriors. They also had excellent fighting traditions. Centuries of combat against the Moors had given Spanish soldiers a reputation for fierceness, even cruelty. When attacked, their usual response was to shout the battle cry *"Santiago y a ellos!"* ("St. James"—the patron saint of Spain—"and at them!") and plunge into a fierce counterattack. The culture of Spain produced bold fighting men who were not afraid to take chances, men who counted on their talents to serve them against all odds.

Hispaniola

Historians do not know how long Pizarro spent in Italy; but he matured and must have improved his diplomacy skills because he would later prove to be a great leader. By 1502, he had returned to Spain, still poor, but willing to risk a new venture. Pizarro chose to travel to the New World. Like many young Spaniards, he had decided that if he could not make his fortune in battle against Europeans, he would try to make it by conquering lands in the New World. That year he sailed for Hispaniola, now divided into Haiti and the Dominican Republic, which was the site of Spain's first colony in the New World. (By a curious coincidence, his cousin and fellow conqueror Hernán Cortés was scheduled to sail on the same ship, but remained in Spain because he was injured.)

17

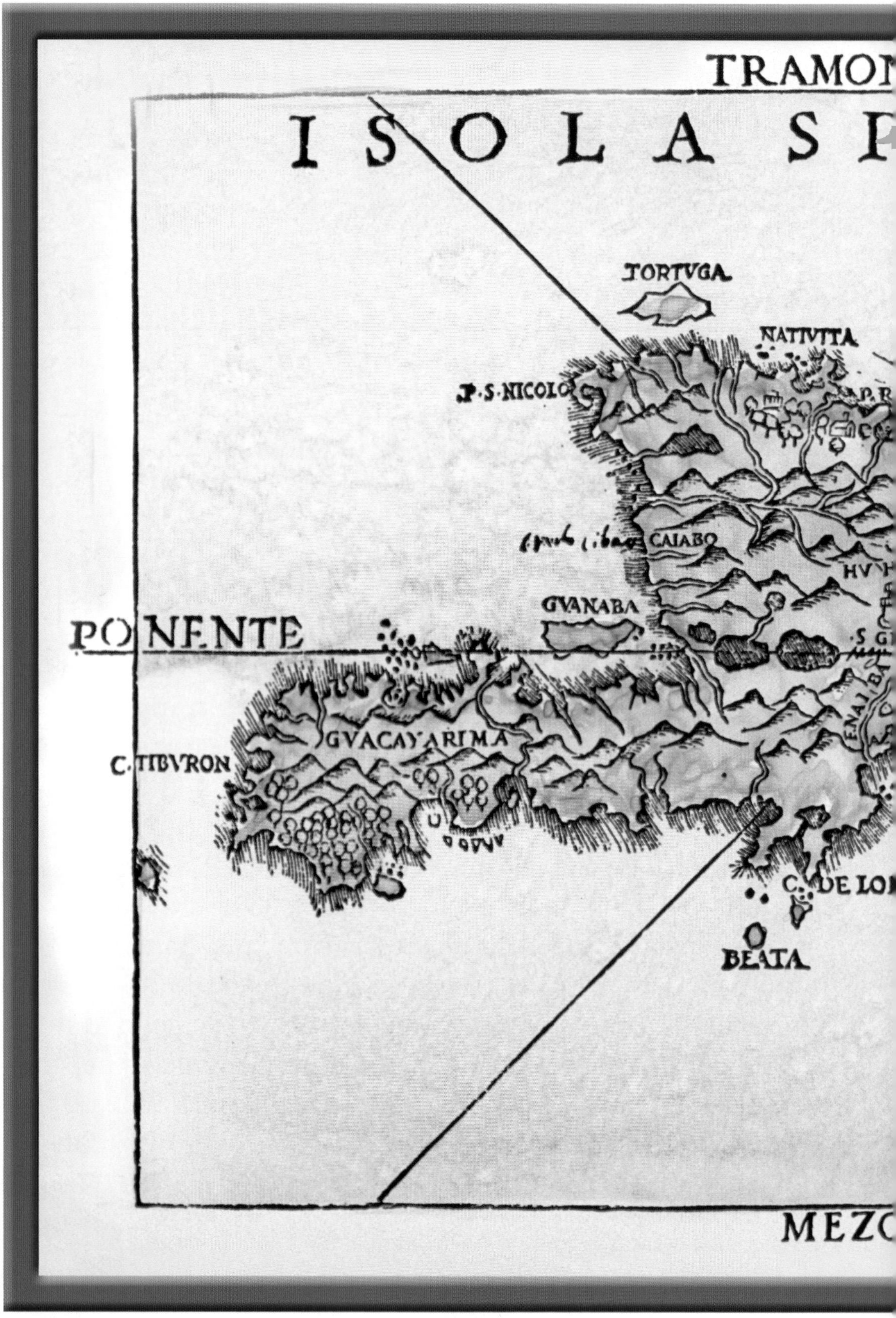

ISOLA SP

TORTVGA

NATIVITA

P.S.NICOLO

P.R

CAIABO

HV H

GVANABA

S G

PONENTE

ENAIB

GVACAYARIMA

C. TIBVRON

C. DE LO

BEATA

AGNVOLA

ISABELLA
VECCHIA

P.PLATA

C.CABRON

XAMANA

IEVANTE

CAIZCI MV

S DOMI
NICO

C.HIGVEY

MONA

SAONA

S.GIOVANNI

In 1492, the same year he "discovered" America, Christopher Columbus landed on the second-largest island in the Caribbean, later named Hispaniola. Lying east of Cuba, it is divided into Haiti to the west and the Dominican Republic to the east. The island is about 400 miles long and 150 miles wide at its widest point. The Spanish killed off the local inhabitants and settled the island with slaves from Africa. The western part of the island, Haiti, was settled by the French and their African slaves, after being ceded to France in 1795. The former slaves of the Spanish rebelled against French rule to form the independent Republic of Haiti in 1804, which split into Haiti and the Dominican Republic in 1843.

For the next seven years, Pizarro was an ordinary citizen of the colony, a respected landowner with few close friends. But already he was displaying the qualities that would allow him to so ruthlessly seize power from the Inca. He could be a loyal friend—while it was good for him. However, if more could be gained by switching sides in a conflict, he would swap loyalties almost without thinking. Still, he had a remarkable ability to convince people, including those people whom he had previously betrayed. Pizarro had the power to win people's trust.

Although Pizarro might have been content to remain an ordinary citizen of Hispaniola for the rest of his days, fate intervened. A man named Alonso de Ojeda, who had sailed with Columbus during his second voyage to America in 1493, had decided to start a colony near present-day northern Colombia. One of the men he took with him was Francisco Pizarro.

Unfortunately, the colony, named San Sebastian, was doomed from the start. The local natives shot poisoned arrows at the Spanish, wounding many of them, including Ojeda. Realizing that San Sebastian needed help, he sailed for Hispaniola, leaving Pizarro in charge.

Alonso de Ojeda is shown in this illustration searching for a lost party. Ojeda began his career as a conquistador with Columbus, but soon began leading his own expeditions. Ojeda pushed to colonize the American mainland at a time when Spanish colonies were on islands. He and Amerigo Vespucci are credited with giving Venezuela ("Little Venice") its name.

Several months passed, and still Ojeda did not return. It was obvious that the colonists had to leave. Pizarro waited until enough of them had died of disease (the mingling of European and American cultures had resulted in outbreaks of deadly diseases such as smallpox and influenza) or arrow wounds so that the survivors could fit in the two ships he had left. Even then, their bad luck did not end; one ship sank, and Pizarro was forced to return to the coast with the survivors. Fortunately, another expedition sent by Ojeda's partner rescued them. They found that the natives had destroyed the few remaining structures of San Sebastian. At this, Ojeda's partner insisted that they found a new colony.

Fortunately, their luck began to change. A young stowaway, Vasco Nuñez de Balboa (another native of Extremadura) knew of a nearby land where the natives did not use poisoned arrowheads. This area was on the Isthmus of Panama, the narrow strip of land between North and South America and home of the present-day Panama Canal. The Spaniards built a town there and elected Balboa their leader. They also helped the local native people fight against another native tribe. As a reward, the local chief gave them some gold.

Eagerly, the Spanish took the gift and immediately asked for more of the precious metal. Laughing, the chief told them that if they traveled over the mountains, they would

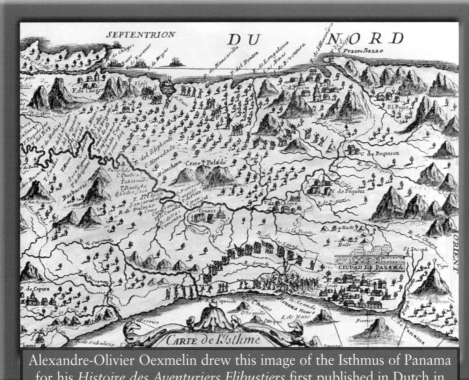

Alexandre-Olivier Oexmelin drew this image of the Isthmus of Panama for his *Histoire des Aventuriers Flibustiers* first published in Dutch in 1678. The English translation was published under the title *The Buccaneers of America*. Oexmelin, also known as John Esquemeling, was a buccaneer (pirate) and a surgeon. The book gives a firsthand account of the sacking of Panama by Henry Morgan in 1671.

find a large ocean and another land where the natives had more gold than even the Spanish could want. The native people of this land reportedly powered their vessels with wind and sails just as the Spanish did.

Balboa and his men were gripped by a frenzy of excitement. They immediately set out to explore this region and to find this great ocean. And without knowing it, they were about to encounter one of the greatest empires in world history.

2

THE SEARCH FOR PERU

Long live the mighty and powerful kings of Castile! In their name I take possession of these seas and regions; and if any prince, be he Christian or infidel, claims any right to these, I am ready to contradict him, and to defend them.
—Vasco Nuñez de Balboa, upon wading into the Pacific Ocean

The Spanish greed for gold was one of the driving forces in their exploration and conquest of the New World. Both the leaders of Spain and the common soldiers hungered after the precious metal. Centuries of fighting the Moors had left the Spanish kings nearly bankrupt. In fact, it was their need for money that led them to support Columbus's wild claim that he knew a shorter route to the East Indies. Even after the establishment of the first few colonies in the New World, the wars Spain fought against the other European kingdoms required more and more gold.

In September 1513, Vasco Nuñez de Balboa climbed alone to the peak of a mountain and for the first time saw the "South Sea" or what is now called the Pacific Ocean. He had set off on an expedition to the Isthmus of Panama in search of a great body of water that he was told about by a Native American. As Balboa and his party crossed the isthmus, they encountered dense jungles, swamps, violent native people, and rough mountainous terrain.

Greed and Betrayal

For the common soldier, gold was very important, too. Many would not have given up a secure life in Spain for the hardships of exploring the New World had they not been promised untold riches. It took a great deal of money to equip oneself as a soldier in the sixteenth century; many of the conquistadors were poor men who had to borrow money to travel to the New World. For them, the gold the natives had found was their just reward for risking their lives in such dangerous expeditions.

Still, the Spaniards' greed made them commit many shocking acts of cruelty and betrayal. If they were also courageous in what they did—the Spanish often fought against the Native Americans at odds approaching 100 to 1—that courage is forever tainted by the fact that so much of it was driven by the lust for a shiny metal.

Balboa's expedition across the Isthmus of Panama is an example of this courage. It was a terrible journey. Mountains had to be crossed, and jungles had to be fought through. The heat of the Tropics tortured the Spanish and ruined their armor and equipment. Many died of disease and exhaustion. It took them twenty-four days to cross forty-five miles of territory. And these hardships were endured only on the mere rumor that there might be gold—and the long-sought route to the East Indies—on the other side.

At the time, it was still not known that the Americas completely blocked the direct sea route to India. Many Spaniards still believed that the Americas were just large islands, not continents, and that the Indies must be somewhere nearby. All that was necessary to reach them was to find the sea route around the American "islands." Ultimately, Balboa believed he was near the Indies when he crossed Panama.

In late September, he and his men stumbled out of the jungle onto the shore of a vast ocean, which stretched as far as the eye could see. Balboa waded into the water, holding a sword and the Spanish flag. He claimed everything that the water touched for the king of Spain and became the first European to touch the Pacific Ocean.

Balboa and his men, including Pizarro, founded a new colony near present-day Panama City. They built ships and sailed along the coastline, finding islands rich with pearl-bearing oysters. They also heard stories about a wealthy empire that lay beyond the mountains to the south. But it was not Balboa's fate to discover that land of wealth.

Under pressure from Ojeda's partners, King Ferdinand had appointed a governor of the colony, Pedro Arias de Avila (usually known as Pedrarias Davila). Jealous of the influence of Balboa, Davila trumped up charges of treason, and had Balboa arrested. The leader of the soldiers who arrested Balboa was none other than

Pedrarias Davila is shown here attacking natives at Darién (the Isthmus of Panama). Davila was governor of the Spanish colony there. He is also known as a mentor to another famous conquistador, Hernando de Soto.

Pizarro, who gladly betrayed the man who had quite probably saved his life. Pizarro's intention was to make a good impression on the new governor for the colony. (Some historians claim that Pizarro was in charge of the men who executed his former friend two years later, in 1519.)

Life as a Colonist

As a reward for his good service, the governor gave Pizarro an *encomienda*, or plot of land, near the site of present-day Panama City. An *encomienda* (also known as a *repartimiento*) was an estate granted by the governor of a Spanish colony. It was basically a grant of land; but any of the Native Americans who lived on that land were expected to work for the person who held it, the *encomendero*, earning a meager wage. While the Spanish government was officially opposed to enslaving the native people of the New World, they did wish to control their future, turning them into working peasants. The government parceled out both the land and the Native Americans to Spaniards, who were then expected to instruct the native people in Christianity and improve their living standards. In order that the encomenderos (the Spanish landowners) not become too powerful, or interfere too much in the lives of the native people, however, the natives were forbidden to live on the Spaniards' land. Moreover, the Spaniards nearly never practiced the high-minded ideals behind the *encomienda* system. They abused the Native Americans, forcing them to work long hours searching for gold that the Spaniards would eagerly take. The Spaniards sometimes took advantage of the Native American women and kept nearly all the food they produced. In many ways, the system was almost worse than slavery.

For Pizarro, however, life was good. He was financially comfortable, if not rich, and was one of the most important colonists in Panama. For the next three years, he seemed content with his life as an important landowner. But by 1522, one of the most crucial years in the history of the New World, events were unfolding that would change his life.

Understanding the New World

The first news came from the north. Pizarro's distant cousin Hernán Cortés seized Mexican territories nearly as large as Spain itself: the Aztec Empire. Landing in present-day Vera Cruz, Mexico, in 1519 with only 400 men, Cortés had, in the span of three years, used diplomacy, deception, and the overwhelming force of the Spanish cavalry to conquer the fierce and warlike Aztecs. Cortés understood that many of the peoples conquered by the Aztecs were eager to rebel against them and would help the Spanish fight. He was smart enough to use the Aztecs against themselves, and his strategy was crucial to his success. Cortés's daring expedition had brought millions of pesos' worth of gold to himself and the king of Spain. Pizarro, who must have made a careful study of the conquest of Mexico, used many of Cortés's techniques during his own daring conquest of the Inca.

The second important event was a sailing expedition, originally led by Ferdinand Magellan, that had managed to find a sea route around the tip of South America and sail completely around the world. Although Magellan had died along the way, his ships eventually returned to Spain, proving without a doubt that the New World was nowhere near the Indies. This caused Davila, who before this had been searching for the nonexistent water route across Panama to the Indies, to give permission for some of his men to sail south in pursuit of Balboa's legends of gold.

One of them, Pascal de Andagoya, landed in what is now Colombia at the end of the year, near the Biru River. Many of the native people there had golden ornaments. The Spanish asked them where they got the gold. Thinking they meant where the native people were from, the natives said Biru, meaning the area near the river. The Spanish mispronounced this as Peru, finally giving a name to the empire of gold they were seeking. Pizarro now decided that he would find this magical land called Peru and conquer it the way Cortés had conquered Mexico and the Aztec Empire.

MEXICO

Legend:
- ← 1519 route
- ◄·· Retreat, 1520
- ← 1521 route
- ▭ Aztec Empire
- ● Town or City
- ▲ Volcano

Lake Texco...

Tenochtitlán ●

PACIFIC OCEAN

N

This map shows the routes Spanish conquistador Hernán Cortés took in his conquest of the New World between 1519 and 1521. In many ways, Cortés's earlier success spawned a greater interest by Pizarro to secure his destiny in the New World.

Cortés

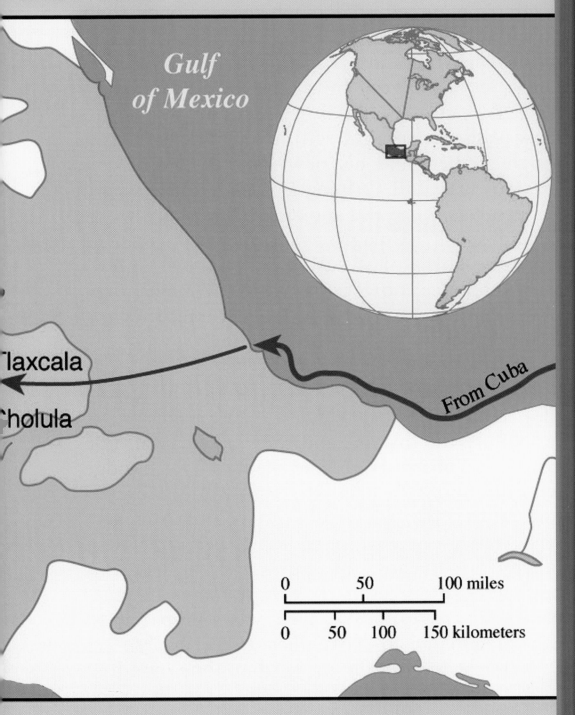

Gulf
of Mexico

Tlaxcala

Cholula

From Cuba

| 0 | 50 | 100 miles |

| 0 | 50 | 100 | 150 kilometers |

The Hungry Harbor

Pizarro's plan required much more money than he alone could gather. Fortunately, he found a natural partner in another Spanish colonist, Diego de Almagro. In many ways they were alike; Almagro could neither read nor write, and he was also born an illegitimate child. He was a tough soldier, like his new partner. But where Pizarro was tall, Almagro was short; where Pizarro was quiet and spoke in a low voice when he did speak, Almagro was loud and given to fearsome bouts of swearing. Their most important difference, however, was that Almagro usually sought to attack a problem directly, while Pizarro was a master of working behind the scenes to get what he wanted.

Together with a priest, Hernando de Luque, they banded together to finance an expedition set to explore the distant land they called Peru. (De Luque was probably just the agent of a local judge who did not want to publicly back the two conquistadors. Still, he kept Pizarro and Almagro, who frequently disagreed, from being at each other's throats until his death.) Even with this pooling of resources, it took more than two years before Pizarro and Almagro were prepared to travel. Finally, in November 1524, Pizarro set forth with little more than one hundred Spaniards like him, each in search of the untold wealth of Peru.

This expedition was not much of a success, however. Pizarro first came ashore near the mouth of the Biru River, but the native people that Andagoya had contacted in 1522 were nowhere to be seen. Pizarro led his force inland, straight into the jungle, but they gave up after several days spent struggling in swamplands and watery bogs.

Once on board the ship, Pizarro and his men had to endure a

Diego de Almagro was one of Pizarro's partners in his conquest of the Inca.

violent storm that nearly wrecked their tiny vessel. Even after that, their luck remained bad. They were sailing along the jungles of present-day Colombia; the terrain everywhere was as bad as the forests along the Biru River. Low on supplies, Pizarro decided to build a camp along the coast and send the ship back for supplies.

Pizarro called the place Puerto Hambre, which means "Hungry Harbor" in Spanish. For more than six weeks, he and his men sat there, waiting for the return of the ship and eating whatever they could catch—mostly seaweed and shellfish. Many of his men died of hunger or from eating poisonous roots. But one day, some found a small village in the jungle. Although the native inhabitants ran away when the Spanish arrived, they soon returned, astonishing the Spaniards with the crude gold ornaments they wore. When asked where the gold came from, they indicated with sign language that it came from the south. It was another clue as to where the land of Peru lay.

Soon afterward, the ship arrived with supplies, and once again Pizarro sailed southward. But he found no other friendly natives like the ones he had met near Puerto Hambre. Several times the Spanish had to fend off attacks, with Pizarro being wounded a few of those times. Finally, he met Almagro, who had followed in his own ship. Natives had also attacked him; an arrow had shot out one of his eyes. But he had found native people with gold who told him about the powerful kingdom that lay somewhere to the south. With their food depleted, the two men decided to return to Panama.

They had not brought much back for their efforts; indeed, they returned from the expedition with fewer men. But with the help of Father de Luque, they convinced the governor to give them permission to set out once again. This time Pizarro was determined to find the wealthy kingdom to the south.

The Quest for Peru

In November 1526, Pizarro, Almagro, and 160 conquistadors sailed south from Panama in two ships. This time they had brought with them the great navigator Bartolomé Ruiz, who decided to travel a different route. He sailed in a southerly direction, straight across the open ocean, which allowed them to sail much faster before turning toward the coast. Ruiz brought them as far south as the San Juan River in southern Colombia. Almagro decided to return to Panama for supplies and reinforcements. Meanwhile, Pizarro marched inland, repeating the folly of his first expedition. Ruiz continued down the coast, reaching as far south as present-day Ecuador. Once there, he encountered the balsa raft (the story that was told at the beginning of this book). It marked the first time a Spaniard and an Incan had met.

Ruiz later met Pizarro, exhausted after several months of being attacked by native people in the jungle. Ruiz led Pizarro farther south, telling him of his encounter. The news was a huge relief. At last, they had definite knowledge of the location of Peru. Even better, Almagro returned shortly thereafter with more supplies and eighty additional men. Once again they sailed in a southerly direction. Along the way, the Spaniards passed large villages, but the

Diego de Almagro and Hernando de Luque came to Pizarro's aid, providing him funding for his plan to move farther into the South American mainland. They established a formal partnership and drew up a contract, which Pizarro and Almagro marked, neither being able to write. Here Pizarro, de Luque, and Almagro are shown drawing up their plans for the conquest of Peru.

native people were decidedly unfriendly. Once they landed with horsemen and were attacked by thousands of warriors. Only the strangeness of the Spaniards' horses, which frightened the native people, saved Pizarro that day.

It was decided to drop Pizarro and his men off on Isla Gallo (Island of the Cock) while Almagro again returned in one of the ships to Panama for supplies. Once more Pizarro and his men suffered through hunger and disease, marooned on a rocky island in the middle of the rainy season. The conquistadors grew angry with Pizarro, so

Pizarro and his men wait on Isla Gallo for the return of Almagro in this image. But they became fearful of the native people on the island, so they built a raft and sailed instead to Gorgona Island, on the Colombian coast.

he sent a few of the crankiest men back to Panama on the other ship.

By now, word about the poor progress of the expedition had reached the new governor of Panama, Pedro de los Rios. At this discovery, he decided not to send Pizarro additional supplies but instead attempted to force him to return to Panama. Pizarro had a difficult choice to make.

On one hand, if he refused to return now, he might be branded a traitor—and even killed—if he survived and returned to Panama later. But on the other hand, he knew that he was closer to Peru. To turn back now seemed senseless, even if the rest of his men thought it was too risky to continue their search. Finally, Pizarro made a momentous decision. He walked down to the beach in front of the men and drew a line in the sand with his sword. The gesture was not merely symbolic. Of those men who would continue the search, those who chose to go with him, he requested that they step to his side of the line. Anyone else who wanted to abandon the search should remain on the other side. In the end, only thirteen men stayed with Pizarro when the ships sailed for Panama.

Meeting the Inca

After making a raft, Pizarro and his men managed to move to Gorgona Island, a more pleasant place to live. All at once, Pizarro's luck turned around. A ship commanded by none other than Ruiz sailed by the island, and Pizarro and his men managed to convince the navigator to take them south. They were now headed to the city of Tumbes, the same city of which the native people on the balsa raft had previously spoken.

In a few short weeks they had arrived there, finally stepping foot into the Inca Empire. The natives of Tumbes treated them with kindness and curiosity; they had never seen anyone with white skin or heavy beards like those of the Spaniards. Nor had they ever seen chickens or pigs; the few Pizarro gave them as a sign of good intentions made them laugh. They were frightened and impressed by the Spaniards' harquebuses. And the Spaniards were impressed by the gold they saw. There was gold on the walls of the temples, gardens with plants made totally of gold, and golden plugs in the ears of the native nobles, some so large that their earlobes nearly touched their shoulders.

Most thrilling to the Spanish were the tales they heard of Cuzco, the capital of the Inca Empire, which was said to be the largest and wealthiest city in the world.

This is a painting of the Inca by an artist in the Cuzco school of art. The term "Cuzco" refers to Peruvian painters of various ethnic origins active in Cuzco from the sixteenth to the nineteenth centuries. Many of their works were painted by Indians who had been taught by Spanish masters such as Loyola. The Peruvians were influenced by Spanish masters impressed with European art, as well as by their own indigenous traditions.

Pizarro and his men sailed a little farther south from Tumbes and then returned to Panama, which they reached near the end of 1527. Because he had been gone for a year and a half, some had thought Pizarro must be dead. But he was very much alive and more satisfied than ever before. He had located Peru, and it was truly the golden empire of his dreams. Immediately Pizarro began planning his next voyage there. This trip would not be one of exploration, however. When Pizarro next set foot in Peru, it would be to conquer it.

3

THE EMPIRE OF THE SUN

Our Father the Sun has revealed to me that after the reign of twelve Incas, his own children, there will appear in our country an unknown race of men who will subdue our Empire. I think that the people who came recently to our own shores are the ones referred to. They are strong, powerful men, who will outstrip you in everything. The reign of the twelve Incas ends with me. I can therefore certify to you that these people will return shortly after I have left you, and that they will accomplish what our father the Sun predicted they would.
—The dying words of Sapa Inca Huayna Capac, 1525

The empire Pizarro set out to conquer was one of the most advanced and successful in the New World. Yet, strangely enough, it had only recently emerged as a major power in the region and, ironically, had reached the height of its power before Pizarro and his men arrived.

The tribe that had built this great kingdom was called the Inca; their ruler was known as the Sapa Inca, or, more plainly, the Inca. He reigned over a group of fierce warriors who had built and organized one of the most unique governments in the history of mankind.

The Making of an Empire

Although the Inca had moved into the Valley of Cuzco, now the home of their great capital, it was previously the site of several other civilizations. The Inca did not expand much beyond that region until the reign of the ninth Sapa Inca, Pachacuti, which began in 1438. For the next sixty years, the soldiers of the Inca Empire greatly expanded their territory under his control.

The two major factors that influenced Incan success were their army and their roadways. The Inca were a fierce and determined warrior people. They had a professional standing army, one that frequently fought and sharpened its skills. This gave them an advantage over many of the tribes with whom they fought, who were disorganized, weak, and poorly outfitted.

The second key to Incan success was their well-built roadways. The Inca had constructed a vast series of causeways that linked every part of the empire, running over the high mountains, through rock cliffs, and, using unstable rope suspension bridges, over the great rivers of the region. A special class of Inca, the *chasqui*, or runners, served as

These are the ruins of Machu Picchu, thought to be a city or a royal estate and religious retreat. It was built by the Inca in the Andes Mountains most likely in the 1400s. It is situated between two sharp peaks at an altitude of 7,710 feet. The Spanish abandoned their search for this "lost city" and it was only in 1911 that U.S. explorer Hiram Bingham discovered the site. One of the few ancient urban centers found nearly intact, it is about five square miles in area, and includes a temple and a citadel, or fortress.

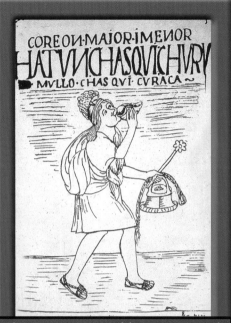

This Incan runner blowing a conch shell and carrying a quipu was drawn by Don Felipe Wamán Poma de Ayala. Poma, who was of mixed Incan and Spanish descent, wrote an illustrated letter to the king of Spain documenting Incan culture and history, as well as Spanish cruelty to the Inca.

messengers over these roads. A message would be recited to the *chasqui* (the Inca never developed writing) who would memorize it before running at top speed to his destination. After about a mile, he would reach a hut containing another *chasqui*. The first messenger would tell the second *chasqui* his message, and when he was done, the second *chasqui* would run down the road until he reached the next hut. Using this system, a message could travel about 150 miles a day, or from the coast of Peru to Cuzco in about three days. (A century later, the Spanish mail would take four or five times as long to travel the same distance.) The system was so efficient that fresh fish could be brought from the coast to the Sapa Inca in Cuzco without spoiling. And the Inca kept barracks for their soldiers filled with food, weapons, and other supplies along the road every few miles. In this way, they could keep their armies moving rapidly wherever they were needed.

Land of the Four Quarters

Although the Inca lacked a writing system, they had designed a unique method of keeping track of dates, numbers, and other information, vital for a government that tried to manage every aspect of the lives of its subjects. This was the *quipu*, or knotted cord. It consisted of a thin rope from which hung small strings of various colors, each one of them tied with tiny knots in various places. The knots were a way of keeping track of numbers; the position of the knot on the cord indicated how big or small the number was. The different colors indicated what kind of number was being stored: numbers representing populations, soldiers, how much food was stored in a given place, and so on. The *quipu* could not speak alone, however. It took a special kind of Incan priest to read it, and even he had to rely on his memory to know exactly what the *quipu* was counting. In this way, the empire functioned for centuries.

The Inca were a religious people, and their entire world centered on their spiritual beliefs. They believed that they were children of the Sun, which they worshiped. Although they had many gods, Inti, the Sun, was their chief. Long ago, he had sent his son, Manco Capac, and his daughter, Mama Ocllo, to the earth to teach the people how to live. Capac and Ocllo, who were husband and wife as well as brother and sister,

49

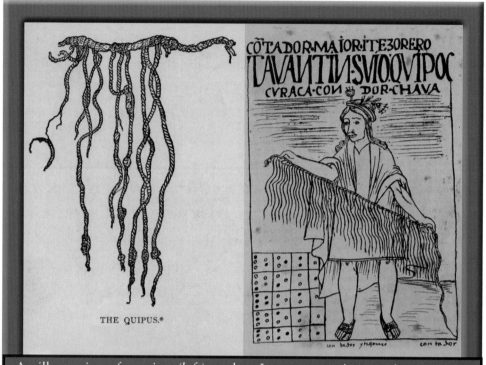

THE QUIPUS.*

CŌTADOR·MAȚOR·ȚTE3ORERO
ȚAVANTȚNSVȚOQVȚPOC
CVRACA·CON DOR·CHAVA

An illustration of a quipu *(left)*, and an Incan man using a quipu to count *(right)*. The Spanish were unable to find a single Incan priest or specialist to decipher any quipus for them.

eventually settled in Cuzco, where they raised the children who would one day be the rulers of the Inca. (In memory of these gods, and for many generations, the Sapa Inca always married his sisters, and his heir had to be his son by his father's sister.) As a way of unifying their empire, the Inca forced the tribes they conquered to worship the Sun. While those tribes could keep their other gods, they had to make the Sun their chief god. The Incas also forced the conquered tribes to speak their language, Quechua, which is still spoken by the Indians of Peru today.

The Sapa Inca controlled every aspect of his subjects' lives, including where they lived, how much land they farmed, and whom they married. The Sapa Inca also made a frequent practice of touring the empire, gathering his subjects to him so that he could decide how they could best serve his needs. In some ways, the system was efficient. Unlike many other parts of the world, including Europe, famine and starvation were almost unheard of in Peru because the Inca kept track of their food and created storehouses of provisions every year. The skilled craftsmen of the empire, many from other tribes that the Inca had conquered, never had to worry about buying their supplies or selling their wares— the government gave them everything they needed and kept everything they made. This also meant that the government was centralized; if for any reason the Sapa Inca was unable to give his orders, the whole system might collapse. Moreover, many of the people the Inca conquered resented this control over their lives. Pizarro, like Cortés before him, was able to exploit this resentment, as we shall see.

Still, the Incan system of government was remarkably advanced for its day. They were careful to keep the people they had conquered under strict control. Each tribe had to wear its own costume so that no one could mistake them for their Incan masters. The Inca also moved whole villages of people into conquered regions, providing safer areas for their armies.

51

Conquered chiefs' sons were also brought to the capital city of Cuzco so that the Sapa Inca had a ready supply of hostages should the newly subdued chiefs plan any rebellion.

Dire Omens and Disease

Under Huayna Capac, the twelfth Sapa Inca, the Inca had conquered as far north as Quito, in present-day Ecuador, and controlled the coast as far south as present-day Chile. The Inca called their empire the "Land of the Four Quarters," but a better translation might be "The World." It seemed to them that they had conquered all of the civilized people in the world; to the south were only deserts; to the north and east impassable jungles; and to the west, the Pacific Ocean. Into that world came bearded white strangers from another world, and nothing was ever the same again.

Like the Sapa Inca before him, Huayna had married his sisters and had sons by them, following Incan customs. One of these boys, Huascar, was chosen to be Huayna's heir. But Huayna's favorite son was Atahualpa, who was not eligible to become the Sapa Inca because he was the son of the daughter of the chief of Quito, which Huayna had conquered. Huayna had fallen in love with this beautiful woman. When she died, he decided to live in Quito rather than Cuzco, in order to be near the place she had once loved.

Huayna Capac was one of the last of the Incan emperors. The Inca Empire reached its greatest extent and power under his rule, but it disintegrated soon after his death. This was delayed by Huayna Capac's decision to divide the empire, leaving Quito to his favorite son, Atahualpa, and not Huascar, son by his chief wife. The war between the brothers was ongoing when Francisco Pizarro began his conquest.

Huayna was troubled by the Spaniards' arrival. There had been many dire omens in recent years that some Inca believed meant the end of the empire. Many of the same Inca believed that the Spanish had come in fulfillment of those prophecies. Some Inca actually believed that the Spaniards were gods, servants of the invisible creator god of the Inca, Viracocha. It is for this reason that the Inca often referred to the Spaniards as *viracochas*.

Huayna did not have much time to meditate on these problems. He died soon after, a victim of an epidemic that swept through the Inca Empire during 1526 and 1527. The illness was probably smallpox, a terrible, disfiguring disease common in Europe but unknown in the Americas. Because many of the Spaniards had been exposed to the disease in their youth, they had already developed immunity to it; but the Native Americans had no such resistance and died in great numbers. Some 200,000 people are thought to have died in the area of Cuzco alone during that time. Huayna's death threw the empire into turmoil. His son Huascar succeeded him as Sapa Inca; but his other son, Atahualpa, was made the ruler of Quito and the bulk of the army remained with him. Tensions between the brothers were high and would soon explode into violence.

Meanwhile, Pizarro returned to Panama and received a warm welcome from the Spanish colonists there, who were excited by the gold he had found. His reception from the governor, however, was cold since he was unhappy with Pizarro's refusal to obey his previous orders to return.

Determined to press forward, Pizarro decided to travel to Spain and plead his case before the king himself.

King Charles I of Spain was also Holy Roman Emperor Charles V of the Hapsburg dynasty. He was initially regarded as a foreigner in Spain even though his mother Joan was the daughter of Ferdinand and Isabella. Under Charles, Spain's empire in the New World gained strength even as he worked to increase his influence throughout Europe.

Permission to Conquer

Pizarro arrived in Spain in 1528 and traveled to Toledo to meet the Spanish king, Charles I. Unlike the governor of Panama, King Charles was very eager to let Pizarro continue his plans of conquest. The memory of Cortés's success in Mexico was still fresh in everyone's mind, and now Pizarro had found another rich kingdom in the New World. King Charles had several reasons to allow Pizarro the risk of conquering the Inca, for he was not just King Charles I of Spain but also the Holy Roman Emperor Charles V, leader of much of Germany and Italy. He dreamed of strengthening his empire and continuing the wars against the Muslims of North Africa, both visions that required great wealth.

Pizarro was given formal permission from the king to raise a small army and conquer Peru. He was also made a knight and given the title of captain-general (overall commander of the armed forces) in Peru for life. He immediately set out to find Spanish volunteers for his expedition. Relatively few Spaniards wanted to go with him as soldiers, but Hernando, and his half brothers Juan and Gonzalo Pizarro, and his mother's son Martin de Alcantra all decided to join Pizarro, companionship that would be important later. Pizarro's young cousin Pedro also joined him. The Pizarros looked after one another; they were all cruel, ruthless men who liked to fight. They each found lying, deception, and betrayal to be as natural as breathing. This talent of deceit undoubtedly helped Francisco Pizarro conquer an empire of millions, however disease-ravaged, with his small army, steady Spanish reinforcements, and Indian allies.

Pizarro and his men returned to Panama in 1530. Once there, Almagro was furious at finding out that Pizarro had already given all the best jobs in the expedition to his brothers. The quarrel, which almost escalated into violence, was finally settled after everyone agreed that Almagro would have his own territory to rule in Peru once it was conquered. Still, the disagreement caused ongoing hatred between Almagro and the Pizarros.

After much hard labor, the expedition of some 200 men, 30 horses, and a few small cannons set sail in three ships from Panama on December 27, 1530. For some reason unknown to anyone but Pizarro himself, the conqueror did not go directly to Tumbes but instead chose to lead his men overland through the dense jungles of modern-day Ecuador. The Spaniards suffered horribly on the journey, contracted native diseases, and had great difficulty cutting their way through the jungles on foot. Even after they left the dense tropical growth, they still found the journey harrowing. While traveling to the island of

This engraving from *Den Vermerdernden Spieghel*, a treatise by Spanish bishop Bartolome de la Casas, depicts the horrors of the Spanish conquest of South America. Spanish conquistadors often slaughtered people throughout the New World and fed them to dogs.

Puna, near Tumbes, they met a representative of the Inca Empire who warned them not to trust its natives, who were cannibals. The Incan man told the Spaniards that the Puna natives were only waiting for the proper moment to strike. Perhaps as a show of good faith to the Inca, Pizarro and his men attacked the Punans in a bloody battle that the Spanish won using their horses and superior weapons.

On May 16, 1532, Pizarro finally crossed into the Inca Empire, landing at Tumbes. Hernando de Soto, another native of Extremadura, brought with him one hundred men, more horses, and two ships that reinforced Pizarro's force. What they found surprised them. Instead of a rich town full of friendly Inca, Tumbes was a burnt-out ruin, plundered of all its treasure. The natives they met tried to attack them but were quickly repelled by the Spanish cavalry. Something had clearly happened there to cause the destruction, but whatever it was remained a mystery to the Spaniards. Pizarro, who could not determine what had caused the ruined vicinity, did not let it stop him from following his plans. He decided to establish a small town, San Miguel de Piura, leaving there some of his less able soldiers. Pizarro, who continued with his army on foot, finally headed for the heartland of the Inca Empire on September 24, with 106 soldiers and 60 horsemen.

The Journey to Cuzco

The land of Peru is divided into three general regions. There is the dry coastal plain, where irrigated waters are channeled to grow crops; the high peaks of the Andes Mountains, arranged in two great chains that run parallel to the South American coastline; and the high and cold altiplano, lands that occasionally dip down into a fertile valley. It was just that type of fertile valley region where the Incan capital of Cuzco was located. As Pizarro and his men marched from the coastal plain toward the Andes, they saw signs of war everywhere. Villages had been destroyed, and men, who had been hanged by their feet, had been left to die. Soon after, the Spanish learned that the cause of the destruction was a civil war between the two sons of Huayna Capac: Atahualpa and Huascar.

For the first few years after the death of Huayna Capac, the brothers' relations had been calm but tense. This situation could not last, however. Atahualpa's control of Quito and the best parts of the Incan army made a mockery of Huascar's claim to be the supreme ruler of the empire. For his part, however, Atahualpa, one of the best Incan generals, may secretly have believed that he would make a better Sapa Inca than his half brother Huascar. Although historians do not know how

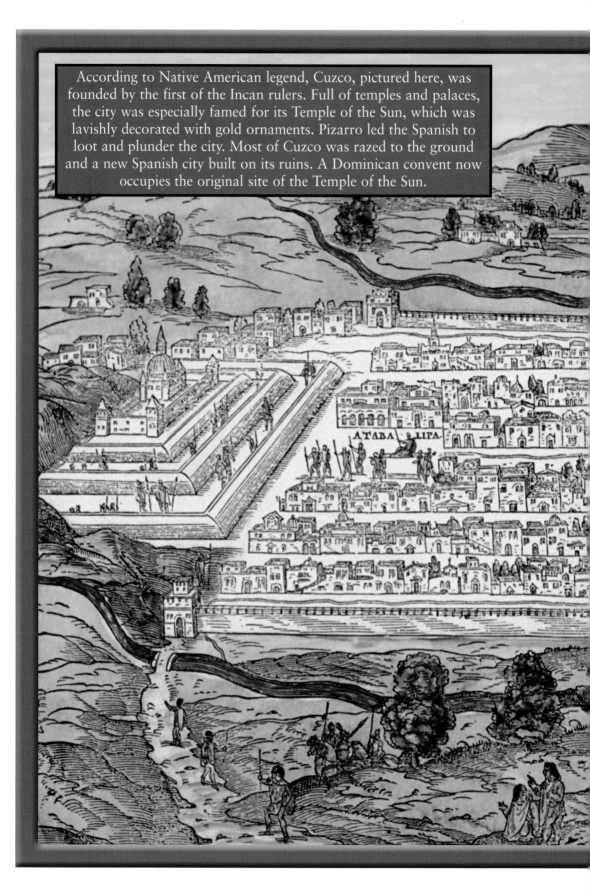

According to Native American legend, Cuzco, pictured here, was founded by the first of the Incan rulers. Full of temples and palaces, the city was especially famed for its Temple of the Sun, which was lavishly decorated with gold ornaments. Pizarro led the Spanish to loot and plunder the city. Most of Cuzco was razed to the ground and a new Spanish city built on its ruins. A Dominican convent now occupies the original site of the Temple of the Sun.

the conflict began, they do know that Huascar sent an army to invade Atahualpa's territory early in 1532.

The troops Huascar used for this invasion were mostly ordinary Inca pressed into service as soldiers. They proved no match for the seasoned veterans of Atahualpa's army, who crushed Huascar's troops in a series of battles. They then marched southward, led by Atahualpa's best generals, Chalcuchima and Quizquiz. Atahualpa defeated Huascar's army outside Cuzco and occupied the city. Huascar was murdered, along with all his relatives.

When it was over, Atahualpa had eliminated much of the Incan royal family and proclaimed himself Sapa Inca, although by tradition he had no real claim to the title. He was resting at Cajamarca, a city in the Andes, on his way to Cuzco, when a messenger brought word that the Spaniards had returned.

Atahualpa immediately made a mistake. Seriously underestimating how powerful Spaniards could be, he invited them to visit him in Cajamarca. He was still more concerned about his recent civil war victory than about the actions of this tiny force of invaders.

Pizarro, though, had fully understood what the civil war might mean for Spain. With discontent brewing throughout the Inca Empire, he might be able to find plentiful allies

After the death of Huayna Capac, his sons Huascar and Atahualpa fought for control of the empire. Huascar was eventually killed on the orders of Atahualpa.

to help him in his conquest of the land, just as Cortés had previously done in Mexico. Pizarro was firmly committed to making Spanish history repeat itself in Peru.

Pizarro traveled with his army for a week. Together they marched over the mountains and the hard stone steps of the Incan roads and past threatening fortresses that were curiously empty of soldiers. (Atahualpa, having decided to allow the Spaniards to come to him, did not post any of his soldiers along the way.) At last, the Spaniards looked down into the wide Valley of Cajamarca. An army of at least 50,000 Inca was camped there with the distant vista of the city's thatched roofs and golden temples. It was Friday, November 15. The following days would change the course of history in the New World forever.

4

THE CONQUEST

But our Lord God permitted that, while this Inca and his cap-
tains were involved in the human massacre that we have seen,
punishment should come for his tyranny and cruelness, for he
fell into the hands of the Spaniards, and he finally paid for
every evil that he had committed.
— Father Bernabe Cobo, *History of the Inca Empire*

Pizarro selected his two most trusted captains,
the two Hernandos—Pizarro, his brother, and
de Soto—to visit with the Sapa Inca. Trying to
look intimidating and impressive, the conquistadors rode to Atahualpa's camp on their horses, fully
dressed in cotton armor. The situation was tense as
thousands of warriors surrounded them, ready to
strike at a word from the Incan emperor.

Meeting Atahualpa

The Spaniards found the emperor sitting on a
stool, surrounded by his followers. None were
permitted to glance at the face of their god-
ruler; in fact, as a sign of submission,
people who visited the Sapa Inca had

Atahualpa underestimated the power, cunning, and greed of the Spanish, who destroyed forever the Incan kingdom.

to place a symbolic burden of sticks on their backs as a token of their submission to his rule. The emperor was wearing a strange hat decorated with a scarlet fringe of string that hung down to his eyebrows; this was the traditional symbol of the Sapa Inca and equivalent to a crown.

Hernando Pizarro explained that he was the brother of the leader of the Spaniards, who came in friendship and wanted the Inca to join him that night for dinner. Atahualpa declined, saying he was fasting; if he lied, it was no greater lie than Pizarro's offer of friendship. De Soto gave a riding demonstration, but if Atahualpa was impressed, he did not show it. The Spaniards and the Inca shared some *chicha*, the Incan beer, and Atahualpa sent them back to the town of Cajamarca with his permission to stay in the houses along the three sides of the town's main square. He also said he himself would visit them the following day.

That night the Spanish were glum. Alone in hostile territory, they seemed to be at the mercy of a man who had just proved himself an able and active general. But Pizarro had a desperate plan, not unlike his cousin Cortés.

When Cortés had first landed in Mexico, his goal was to somehow maneuver his way into the capital city of Tenochtitlán without fighting a battle against the Aztecs. Gathering allies among the Aztecs, who had begun to hate their leaders, he had succeeded in entering Tenochtitlán but then found himself in the same position as Pizarro did now, surrounded in hostile territory and at the mercy of a warrior-king. Cortés's daring solution was to go to the Aztec emperor, Montezuma, and offer him a choice: either come with the Spanish to their quarters as their hostage, or be killed immediately. His audacity was rewarded. Montezuma came with the Spaniards, and for several months, Cortés virtually ruled the kingdom, using Montezuma to issue his orders. Pizarro intended to duplicate his cousin's feat by using Atahualpa, the newly self-declared Sapa Inca.

Montezuma, the ninth Aztec king, meets with Hernán Cortés. In 1502, Montezuma succeeded his uncle Ahuitzotl as the leader of an empire that had at the time stretched from Mexico to the borders of Guatemala. Caught between his religious faith and his discontented people, Montezuma was unable to put up a sustained resistance against the Spanish invasion.

Pizarro arranged his cavalry and soldiers carefully. The houses in which they were staying were surrounded on three sides by the main square and closed on the fourth side with a gate. Pizarro now stationed his men inside the houses: the cavalry on two sides, ready to charge out into the square, and the infantry along the third wall. Two falconets, or small cannons, covered the square. When the cannon fired, the rest of the Spanish would attack.

That Saturday dragged on slowly for the terrified Spaniards. Not until that afternoon did Atahualpa, along with his army, begin to approach the town. At one point, he stopped and sent a message to the Spaniards that he would come the following day. Pizarro returned the message telling him that he had nothing to fear. Hearing this, Atahualpa changed his mind again. He would come without his warriors, bringing instead some 6,000 *orejones* to attend him.

Courage and Bloodshed

The sun was setting when he finally arrived, filling the square with his many servants. To his surprise, Pizarro was not waiting there to meet him. Instead, a priest, Father Vincente de Valverde, emerged and began to lecture the Sapa Inca, supreme ruler of the mightiest empire in the New World, the descendent of the Sun god himself, on the Catholic religion.

Father Valverde, via a translator, launched into a brief history of the world, according to sixteenth-century Christians. He explained how God had created men to serve him. The pope, God's representative on Earth according to the Catholic Church, had decreed that the people of this part of the world were to be ruled by the Spanish. If they submitted and agreed to be ruled by the king of Spain, there would be no bloodshed. Otherwise, the Spanish would attack them ruthlessly—and only the Inca would be to blame.

This was a version of the famous *requirimiento*, a document that the king of Spain ordered be read to the native people of the New World before any fighting took place. Atahualpa was gravely insulted. He asked to see the prayer book that Valverde was holding, since the priest claimed it stored the holy knowledge he would need for everlasting life. Glancing at its pages, he then threw it away.

Valverde was mortified. Afraid for his life, the priest ran back to the Spaniards, begging them to punish the blasphemous Inca. And at a signal from Pizarro, they attacked.

Sapa Inca Atahualpa is shown listening to Father Valverde's speech—more of an ultimatum—on behalf of the Spanish king to submit to the Spanish Crown and convert to Catholicism or perish. After the speech, the Spanish ambushed the Incan delegation and captured Atahualpa.

It was a slaughter. Dead bodies quickly blocked the gateway to the square, and the rest of the Inca had nowhere to run. Spanish cavalry devastated them, slicing them with their swords, while crossbow bolts and bullets whizzed across the square. Meanwhile, Pizarro and his men cut their way toward Atahualpa, who was supported on a litter (a platform between long poles designed to be carried by servants—for the Sapa Inca's feet could never touch the ground). His many attendants died bravely trying to save their emperor, taking up the litter in turn as each man fell, but it was not enough. The Spanish dragged Atahualpa from the litter and carried him back with them. The absolute ruler of Peru was now a prisoner of Spain.

Some 2,000 Inca are said to have died that day, while the only Spaniard to be wounded was Pizarro himself. He had been cut on the hand while he prevented a soldier from killing Atahualpa. Like Cortés, who had slaughtered thousands of Aztecs in the city of Cholula in 1521, Pizarro had done much the same thing just eleven years later.

Pizarro was a cruel and ruthless man, one who thought nothing of killing thousands of people or betraying a loyal friend. But Pizarro and his brothers, especially Hernando Pizarro, were also masters of manipulating their enemies into becoming their friends. This is what Pizarro did to Atahualpa. The Spaniards treated him with courtesy; his family was allowed to live with him, and he was well fed and comfortable. The Sapa Inca proved to be quite clever, too, quickly learning Spanish well enough to speak with his captors and develop a strong chess game. He was even strategic enough to beat the Spaniards, who had been playing the game for years. But being imprisoned infuriated Atahualpa, so he began to devise a plan to get himself out of this predicament.

A Roomful of Gold

Knowing of the Spaniards' lust for gold—mystifying to the Incas, who had no money and valued gold only for its beauty—Atahualpa offered to pay the Spaniards in gold to let him go free and leave his empire in peace. He then offered a ransom he thought would satisfy even the greediest of Spaniards: He would fill a large room in his palace in Cajamarca once entirely with gold and twice with silver.

Pizarro could not believe his ears. Perhaps he doubted the Inca could even supply him with that much precious metal. But with nothing to lose, he agreed to the proposal. They agreed that if the gold could be delivered within the span of two months, then Atahualpa would be released.

In each of their villages the Inca built a temple to the Sun, their chief god. All of these temples were modeled after the main Temple of the Sun in Cuzco. The sun god, Inti, was represented by a golden disc with a human face. After the Spanish conquest, the Inca were forbidden from practicing their religion, leading to its eventual demise.

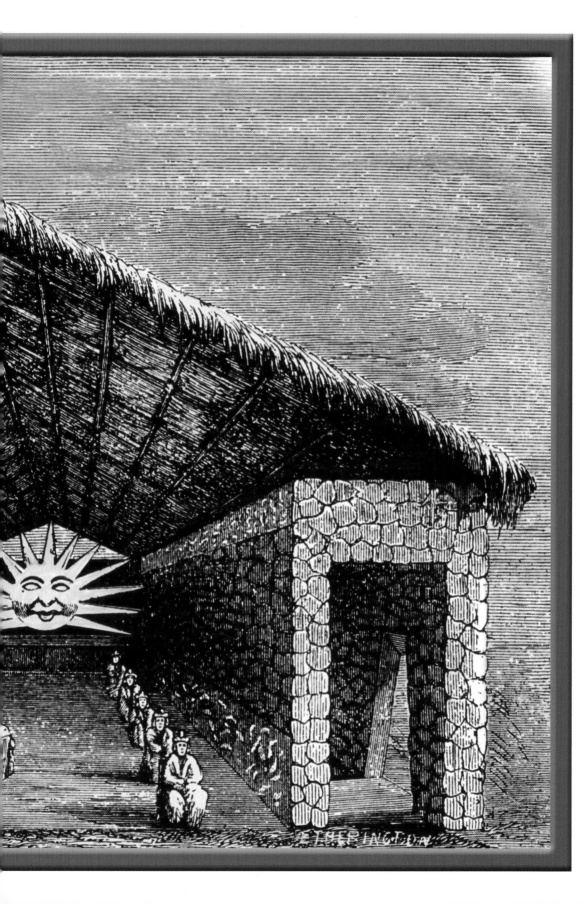

Naturally, Pizarro sent men to certify that the Inca were living up to their word. Strangely enough, the men he sent were both of Atahualpa's great generals, Chalcuchima and Quizquiz, who were under orders from the Sapa Inca not to attack the Spanish. While this order was in place, the Spaniards felt powerless. They sent scouts ahead to Cuzco, and what they found there amazed them.

Cuzco was a massive city made entirely of stone, except for the roofs of buildings, which were covered with thatched straw. Some of the temples were made with stone blocks that had been carefully cut without iron tools or wheels. The masonry abilities of the Inca were amazing; they moved huge boulders and skillfully fitted them into walls. Without using either cement or mortar, these blocks were so well fitted that even today it is not possible to slip a knife blade between them.

But what most interested the Spanish was the Incan gold. The Great Enclosure, which held the Temple of the Sun, had walls plated with solid gold, as were the walls of the temple itself. Inside the enclosure was a garden made of pure gold—golden plants, golden llamas, even golden herdsmen for the llamas. The metal the Spaniards prized was everywhere in Cuzco, and the sight of it took their breath away.

Gold continued to accumulate at Cajamarca, and it was apparent that Atahualpa was going to keep his promise. Pizarro, however, had no such intentions. Meanwhile, Diego de Almagro, Pizarro's partner, had arrived with 150 men and was pressuring Pizarro to distribute the gold. Eventually the estimated $1.4 billion worth of Incan gold was melted down and given out to the men: over 13,000 pounds of gold and 26,000 pounds of silver in total, a staggering sum. One-fifth of the loot was given the royal seal; marking it for King Charles. But there was enough left that even the foot soldiers could expect to get nearly fifty pounds of gold each.

This is a gold statuette of a female goddess. Spanish furnaces worked day and night to melt treasures like these into bullion. The Inca, who treasured gold for its beauty, not value, found this materialistic love for gold repulsive. Don Felipe Wamán Poma included a cartoon in his sixteenth-century book showing the Sapa Inca asking a Spaniard: "Do you actually eat this gold, then?" and the Spaniard replying, "Yes, we certainly do!"

Almagro's men, however, did not get what they had coming. Rather than the equal share they had been promised, Pizarro gave them only 100 pesos each since they had not helped him capture Atahualpa. It was agreed, however, that Almagro was to explore the lands south of Cuzco and could keep whatever he found there.

As for Atahualpa, his usefulness to Pizarro was rapidly decreasing. A month after the treasure had been distributed, the Spaniards accused the Sapa Inca of treason. Atahualpa had rebelled against Huascar and put him to death. A kangaroo court (a mock court where laws are disregarded) of Pizarro, Almagro, and Father Valverde soon found Atahualpa guilty and sentenced him to death, too. The leader was to be burned alive.

This distressed the Inca, who mummified their rulers when they died and even exhibited mummies for religious ceremonies. If Atahualpa was burned to death, his body could not be mummified. Father Valverde gave him a compromise: If he converted to Christianity, he would not be burned. Atahualpa agreed to convert. The leader was given a hasty baptism right before his execution in July 1533. The Spanish strangled Atahualpa to death by placing him in a chair and gradually tightening a thick rope around his neck, a process called garrotting.

Having stripped the Incan capital of all its gold, the Spanish decided to execute the Incan emperor Atahualpa by burning him at the stake. Faced with certain death, Atahualpa begged the same fate that he heard the Aztec ruler Montezuma had faced, death by strangling. That way his body would be preserved for funeral rituals, such as mummification, and the afterlife.

The City of Kings

Pizarro quickly found a new puppet ruler, Tupac Huallca, and began to march on to the Incan city of Cuzco. Unfortunately, Tupac died along the way. At the same time, the Inca who were still loyal to Atahualpa began attacking the Spaniards, who emerged victorious each time. Meanwhile, Pizarro was finding allies among the conquered peoples of the Inca Empire: the Huanca and the Cañari, tribes who welcomed the Spanish as their liberators.

Soon more good fortune came to Pizarro. A young brother of Huascar, Manco, had somehow escaped being murdered by Atahualpa's men. He came to the Spaniards just before they reached Cuzco and asked for their help in putting him on the throne. Pizarro was delighted; the young man seemed eager to cooperate with him and might make an excellent puppet ruler.

Precisely one year after first arriving in Cajamarca, on November 15, 1533, Pizarro and his men arrived in Cuzco. They supervised the coronation of Manco as Sapa Inca, then almost immediately began to strip the city of its remaining treasure. They assisted Manco in conquering the last of Atahualpa's generals, Rumiñavi, and reconquered Quito and the northern provinces of the Inca Empire in the summer of 1534. Now Pizarro began to break up his forces.

Hernando Pizarro was sent back to Spain to bring King Charles the news of his brother's successful expedition. The king was very pleased. He made Pizarro a marquis, one of the highest levels of Spain's nobility, and gave him much of central Peru as his own personal territory.

Almagro and his men, supported by thousands of native porters, set out to explore the territory to the south of Cuzco, present-day Chile. Francisco Pizarro and most of his men returned to the coast, where on January 6, 1535, they founded a new capital for Peru—Ciudad de los Reyes, on the Rimac River—but it soon became known by its present name, Lima, or the City of Kings.

Revolt of the Inca

Gonzalo and Juan Pizarro remained in Cuzco with about a hundred men—and Manco. Bullies and thugs, the two Pizarro brothers soon made the situation intolerable for Manco. They continued to plunder his beautiful capital. They mistreated him, at one point putting him in chains. They took his favorite wife away from him for their own pleasure. These abuses strengthened Manco's resolve to fight the Spanish invaders. By October of that year he tried to escape, but he was soon caught. The Pizarro brothers tortured him and threw him into prison. Only the return of Hernando Pizarro from Spain ended

This plan for the layout of the streets of Lima was drawn in 1674. Much of the chart has faded, making it difficult to read, but the general plan is visible, as are the ornate decorations accompanying it.

Manco's suffering. Still, he did not forgive the Spaniards for their ill treatment of him. He planned his next escape more carefully.

Around Easter of 1536, Manco came to Hernando with a tempting offer: If the marquis' brother would let him go to pray at a shrine in the country, he would return with the idol itself: a life-sized statue of Huayna Capac that was made of solid gold. Hernando, thinking the Inca had been completely subdued by the Spanish, agreed, sending only two guards with the newest puppet emperor. Manco, however, soon slipped away. The Sapa Inca went to meet the troops he had secretly summoned to the Valley of Cuzco.

This 1845 painting by Sir John Everett Millais depicts Pizarro seizing the Sapa Inca of Peru.

Manco made a solemn pledge to remove every Spaniard in Peru. His men quickly encircled Cuzco and Lima. Soon, the Spanish inside Cuzco were suffering terribly. The Inca deliberately set fire to the roofs of the buildings in the city and food was vastly depleted, leaving the Europeans starving. Even their cavalry could not protect them. The Inca boldly threw themselves at the Spaniards' horses, injuring and killing themselves in exchange for wounding the animals. They attacked from the high walls of the houses in Cuzco, out of reach of the Spanish. Even lacking bows or guns, they could do fearsome damage with their slings, which hurled baseball-sized rocks with such force that they could crack a person's skull from 100 feet away. But Manco held back from the final assault on Cuzco. He wanted to wait until all his forces had arrived so that he could descend upon the Spanish in one fell swoop.

The most important asset the Inca had was their fortress of Sacsahuaman, an enormous complex of stone that had three separate and towering walls surrounding it. The Spanish decided to assault this fort, though it would be an incredibly tough battle. Juan Pizarro led fifty horsemen to attack it, but they failed. After being mortally wounded by a rock that hit his head during the assault, he died that night.

Spanish soldiers face a barrage of rocks and stones as they try to battle their way into the Incan fortress of Sacsahuaman.

Hernando Pizarro renewed the attack the following day. The Spaniards, who used the knowledge that European armies had accumulated over the centuries of attacking castle walls, knew exactly what they needed to do. They built tall ladders and used them to climb over the walls of the fortress. After a day-long struggle, they succeeded in capturing it.

Manco's army was composed mainly of peasant soldiers, who would have to return to their fields if there was to be enough food for the coming year. Meanwhile, the Spaniards had defeated his other army outside Lima. Reinforcements were pouring into the new capital from every corner of the Spanish Empire, as hundreds were attracted by the dream of sudden wealth. While Manco managed to continue the siege of Cuzco, every day fewer and fewer soldiers remained available to him. Then in April 1537, Almagro returned from present-day Chile with his army. Manco and his remaining troops eventually fled into hiding. The Incan rebellion had failed.

5

THE NEW EMPIRE

The Spaniards did more harm in four years than the Incas had done in four hundred.

—Spanish official in Peru

Diego de Almagro's expedition to present-day Chile had been a disaster. He had not found any golden cities, just deserts, mountains, and hostile natives. The only thing he had accomplished was killing several thousand of his native porters, who were cruelly mistreated by the Spanish. The Spanish even made them carry their horses to keep the animals from wearing out while traveling the mountainous terrain.

Like other Spanish conquistadors, Pizarro was ruthless in his quest for gold and glory. Through his determined onslaught, Spain defeated the vast Incan Empire, securing most of South America for itself. Although Pizarro had proven himself an able leader, the Inca Empire had been divided in half prior to his arrival, weakening its leadership and stability. Further, silent killers such as European diseases like smallpox, unknown in the Americas before 1492, had eliminated the Native American population in a dramatic way like nothing else could have done.

Pizarro, Ruler of Peru

Almagro was on his way back to Cuzco when he heard about the Incan revolt. He rushed back to the Inca capital. This was partly because he was involved in a dispute with the Pizarros as to who was the rightful ruler of Cuzco. The Pizarros claimed that it was located in the part of Peru given to them by the king, while Almagro's men maintained that it was in his section. The first thing Almagro's men did in Cuzco was capture the other Spaniards, including the Pizarro brothers. That July, they defeated another group of Spaniards loyal to Pizarro. Almagro began to prepare his plan: He would head for the coast, capture Lima, and establish himself as the sole Spanish ruler of Peru.

Francisco Pizarro, however, had other plans. In November 1537, he met with Almagro and agreed to let him have Cuzco until the king decided the matter formally. But almost immediately, his brother Hernando, who had been released by Almagro as part of their bargain, began putting together an army to launch a counterattack on Almagro.

That battle began on April 25, 1538, at Las Salinas, outside Cuzco. Almagro was defeated and arrested. Charges of rebellion were brought against him, and Hernando Pizarro himself tried him. Almagro's sentence was death by beheading, which was carried out on the night of July 8. Francisco Pizarro was now, without any rivals, the Spanish ruler of Peru.

Manco, the Sapa Inca, however, remained free. He brought his remaining followers to Vilcabamba, a city about 100 miles from Cuzco over the Andes Mountains, in a sub-tropical forest. From there he continued a guerilla war against the Spanish invaders. An invasion led by Gonzalo Pizarro in 1539 failed to capture the elusive Inca. Although his situation seemed hopeless, Manco continued to fight, training his men in Spanish combat methods (including using horses) and always searching for the chance to launch another uprising.

This is all that remains of the ruined Incan settlement of Huinay Huayna in Cordillera Vilcabamba, Peru. The Inca built their cities and fortresses on the highlands and steep slopes of the Andes Mountains. Stone steps led up to the top of the cities, which once consisted of stone houses and religious buildings. The blocks of stones weigh several tons and are tightly joined.

Francisco Pizarro was not allowed to enjoy his rule over Peru for very long. Already there were problems with the Spanish government. Hernando Pizarro had returned to Spain in 1539 to attempt to explain why a Spaniard had fought other Spaniards in Peru, but he found that the king was rapidly losing patience with the entire Pizarro clan. He had Hernando arrested for the execution of Almagro and imprisoned in the La Mota Castle until such time as the king thought he should be allowed to go free—this turned out to be 1560, by which time the Pizarro star had fallen far indeed.

To Live and Die by the Sword

First to go was the marquis himself. Almagro's followers, who called themselves "The Men of Chile," had never forgiven Francisco Pizarro for killing their leader. They conceived a plot to kill him and put Almagro's son by a native woman, Diego, in power. On June 26, 1541, after waiting

This engraving illustrates the beheading of Gonzalo Pizarro at Cuzco. The Spaniards in Peru were angered by the publication of regulations from Spain, which put a check on their exploitation and oppression of the native people. The Spaniards in Peru called upon Gonzalo to lead them in a revolt against Spain. He was soon acclaimed as governor of Peru. In 1548, Spain sent Pedro de la Gasca to retake Peru from Gonzalo, who surrendered to him. Gonzalo defended himself as having been selected by the people to lead Peru. He claimed that since it was his family who had conquered the kingdom, he had a right to govern. Gasca had Gonzalo beheaded, ending the reign of the Pizarros in South America.

Engraved for
Moore's Voyages
and Travels.

Gonzalo Pizarro
BEHEADED
at Cuzco.

for hours for Pizarro to attend mass at the Spanish church so that they could attack him on his way, they burst instead into the marquis' house with their swords drawn. Pizarro, who was too arrogant to even have a bodyguard, fled deeper into the house while his servants fought to the death to protect him. The Men of Chile finally caught up with him before he could get his armor on. Fearless as always, however, he drew his sword and fought with the assassins, killing two of them before falling to his own death. The Men of Chile then proclaimed Diego the new governor of Peru.

Their rebellion did not last. The king had already sent an official to investigate conditions in Peru, and he quickly organized an army that crushed the rebels. This brought a period of peace to the area until 1542, when King Charles, influenced by religious leaders who were appalled by the treatment of the Native Americans in the New World, abolished the encomienda system. Resentment among the Spanish settlers of Peru grew until 1544, when Gonzalo Pizarro led them into open revolt. Defeating the small loyalist forces, he ruled Peru as its governor until 1548. At that time, he was defeated and executed by forces led by the king's newly appointed governor. But one consequence of the revolt was that the *encomienda* system was restarted. It did not end until Peru overthrew Spanish rule in the nineteenth century.

The revolt by the Men of Chile had actually helped the Spanish in one way: It brought about the death of Manco. Some of Almagro's followers had fled to Vilcabamba after the victory of the king's forces. They stayed with the exiled Inca, teaching his men Spanish fighting techniques. But in 1544, a new governor of Peru arrived, convincing Gonzalo to start his rebellion. The Spaniards living with Manco decided to see if the new governor would pardon them for rebelling against Pizarro. To make sure they would have his favor, they brutally stabbed Manco to death during a game of horseshoes. Although the Inca killed the assassins, it was too late. Manco was dead, and with him the hope for a revolt by the Inca died as well. Although there were two more Sapa Incas after him, neither were excellent leaders.

The Legacy of Francisco Pizarro

Francisco Pizarro rose from obscurity to rule one of the mightiest empires on Earth. He did this by often acting in the most brutal manner possible, torturing and murdering his enemies, and frequently betraying his friends. He was a great leader and swordsman but, curiously enough, a poor horseman. Yet there was still another less obvious fact about Pizarro's character, something that made him more than a common thug as each of his brothers was, an indefinable trait that allowed him victory against incredible odds.

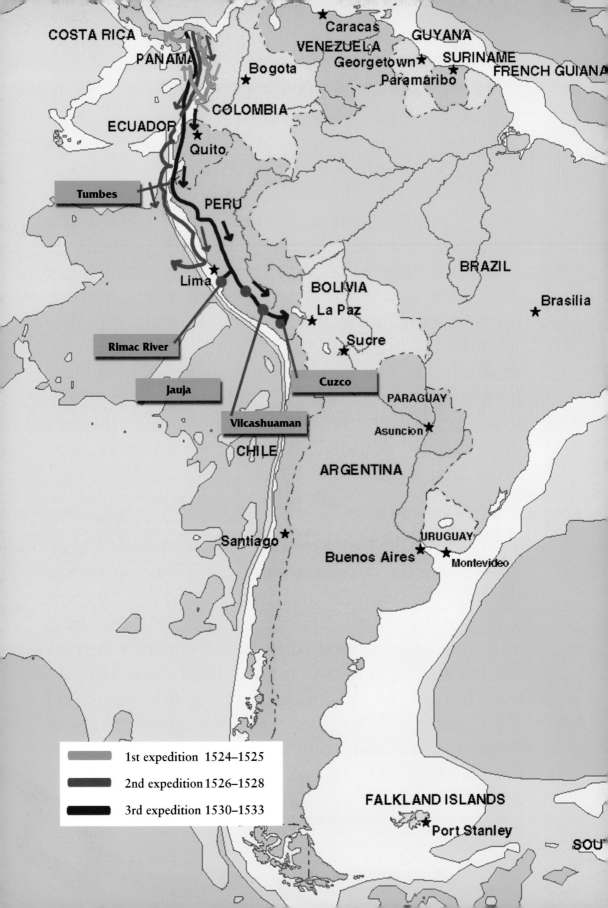

COSTA RICA

PANAMA

VENEZUELA
Caracas

GUYANA

Bogota
Georgetown
SURINAME

Paramaribo
FRENCH GUIANA

COLOMBIA

ECUADOR

Quito

Tumbes

PERU

BRAZIL

Brasilia

Lima

BOLIVIA
La Paz

Rimac River

Sucre

Jauja

Cuzco

PARAGUAY

Vilcashuaman

Asuncion

CHILE

ARGENTINA

Santiago

URUGUAY

Buenos Aires

Montevideo

FALKLAND ISLANDS

Port Stanley

SOU

1st expedition 1524–1525

2nd expedition 1526–1528

3rd expedition 1530–1533

ATLANTIC

OCEAN

GUINEA BISSAU · GUINEA · NIGERIA · Abuja
Conakry · BENIN · GHANA · TOGO
Freetown · IVORY COAST · Porto Novo
SIERRA LEONE · Lome · CAMEROON
Monrovia · Accra · Yaound
LIBERIA · Abidjan · EQUATORIAL GUINEA
SAO TOME & PRINCIPE · Libreville
GABON
Brazzav
Lua

N

Cape T

GEORGIA ISLA

This map shows the three routes Pizarro took through Central America
and down the South American coastline on his three voyages.

This monument to Pizarro was erected in Spain in 1927. The horse's raised leg indicates that Pizarro suffered battle wounds.

Pizarro was a lucky man. At each moment during his various expeditions to Central and South America, when he stood on the brink of disaster and death, his luck allowed him to carry on safely. And no greater good fortune could have happened to him than to arrive in Peru during one of the most vicious civil wars in its history. The collapse of the Incan government allowed Pizarro to befriend the various conquered peoples of the Inca Empire, which helped even the very long odds against him.

Part of Pizarro's good fortune, however, was not due to mere fate, however. The kidnapping of Atahualpa was a stroke of boldness that perhaps only Pizarro could have achieved. Once the Sapa Inca was his prisoner, Pizarro was able to get whatever he wanted from his subjects. He made certain not only to steal all the treasure of the Inca Empire but also to take steps to make sure that it could never rise again. During the

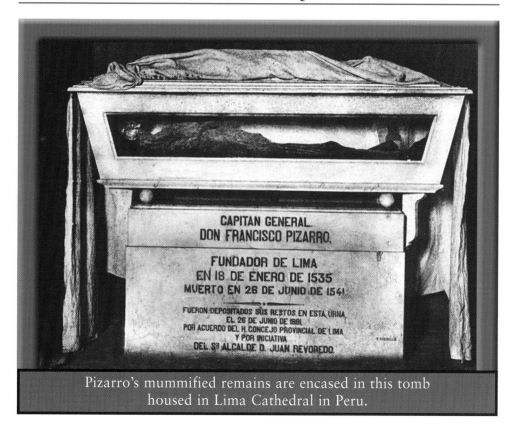

Pizarro's mummified remains are encased in this tomb housed in Lima Cathedral in Peru.

rebellion led by Manco and the civil war against Almagro that followed, Pizarro never lost his motivation, always capitalizing on every situation until he had utterly defeated his enemies.

Pizarro was a rough and violent man, and he was a poor governor. It is perhaps fitting that he died cruelly by the sword—a soldier like him could probably expect no other way of dying. But his true legacy is not only his audacity and courage, but also the destruction of a culture and the enslavement of its people for hundreds of years.

CHRONOLOGY

1475   Francisco Pizarro is believed to be born in Trujillo, Extremadura, Spain.

1502   Pizarro travels to the West Indies with the new governor of Hispaniola, Nicolás de Ovando.

1509   Pizarro joins Alonso de Ojeda's expedition to the Gulf of Urabá, northern Colombia.

1513   Pizarro becomes captain of Vasco Nuñez de Balboa's discovery expedition across Darién, or present-day Panama.

1521   Hernán Cortés conquers the Aztec Empire for Spain.

1524–1525   Pizarro obtains permission for his own expedition to Peru, but because of starvation and conflicts with the native people, it comes to an abrupt end.

1524–1528 Smallpox epidemic in Peru.

1526–1528 Pizarro's voyage of the South American coastline to present-day Ecuador.

1528 Pizarro receives permission to conquer Peru from Spain's King Charles I. He is knighted and named a marquis.

1530–1533 Pizarro sails to Tumbes but is forced to dock at San Mateo Bay because of bad weather.

1531–1533 Measles epidemic in Peru.

1532 Pizarro founds the Spanish town of San Miguel de Piura.

1533 Pizarro arrives in Cuzco and later executes the leader of the Inca, Atahualpa.

1535 Pizarro founds the City of the Kings, present-day Lima, Peru.

1536–1537 The revolt of the Inca.

1541 Pizarro is murdered by the Men of Chile in Lima.

GLOSSARY

cavalry   A group of soldiers mounted on horses.

chasqui   Incan messengers who ran short distances at top speed before giving the message to the next messenger.

conquistador   A Spanish soldier who explored and conquered regions of the New World.

harquebus   A primitive firearm carried by the Spanish during the conquest of Mexico. It used a burning piece of cord or fuse called a match to set off the gunpowder; for this reason, this kind of firearm is called a matchlock.

Hispaniola   A large island in the Caribbean, site of the first Spanish colony in the New World, Santo Domingo. The present-day nations of Haiti and the Dominican Republic are on Hispaniola.

Inca A tribe from the Cuzco Valley in present-day Peru; rulers of a vast empire that included most of present-day Ecuador, Peru, and parts of Chile.

Inti The Incan Sun god, their supreme deity.

Islam A religion founded by the prophet Muhammed; followers of Islam worship one god, called Allah, as the sole deity.

marquis A noble title, usually considered above a baron or lord.

Moors Muslim invaders of Spain from North Africa.

Muslim A member of the Islamic religion.

New World The Americas; the "new world" that Columbus "discovered" in 1492.

orejone A Spanish word for "big ears"; a member of the noble class of the Inca Empire. The name comes from the gold plugs worn in their ears, which sometimes caused their earlobes to drop down to their shoulders.

Peru   The name the Spanish used for the land of the Inca Empire; probably a mispronunciation of the name of the Biru River in Colombia.

quipu   A knotted cord used by the Inca to help remember important numbers.

requerimiento   The Spanish document the conquistadors were legally bound to read before fighting the native people of America. It explained the basics of the Christian religion and told the native people that they must accept the rule of the king of Spain.

Sapa Inca   The supreme and absolute ruler of the Inca Empire.

FOR MORE INFORMATION

American Museum of Natural History
Central Park West at 79th Street
New York, NY 10024-5192
(212) 769-5606
Web site: http://www.amnh.org

The Smithsonian Institution: The National Museum of
     Natural History
Tenth Street and Constitution Avenue NW
Washington, DC 20560
(202) 357-2700
Web site: http://www.mnh.si.edu

Web Sites

Due to the changing nature of Internet links, the Rosen
Publishing Group, Inc., has developed an online list of
Web sites related to the subject of this book. This site
is updated regularly. Please use this link to access
the list:

http://www.rosenlinks.com/lee/frpi/

FOR FURTHER READING

Baquedano, Elizabeth. *Eyewitness: Aztec, Inca & Maya*. New York: DK Publishing, 2000.

Bergen, Lara Rice. *Travels of Francisco Pizarro*. Austin, TX: Raintree Steck-Vaughn, 2000.

DeAngelis, Gina. *Francisco Pizarro and the Conquest of the Inca*. Broomall, PA: Chelsea House Publishers, 2000.

Malpass, Michael A. *Daily Life in the Inca Empire*. Westport, CT: Greenwood Press, 1996.

Manning, Ruth. *Francisco Pizarro (Groundbreakers)*. Portsmouth, NHx Heinemann Library, 2001.

Martell, Hazel Marry. *Civilizations of Peru Before 1535*. Austin, TX: Raintree Steck-Vaughn Publishers, 1999.

Nishi, Dennis. *The Inca Empire (World History Series)*. San Diego, CA: Lucent Books, 2000.

BIBLIOGRAPHY

Bernard-Munoz, Carmen. *The Incas: People of the Sun.* New York: Harry N. Abrams, 1994.

Cobo, Bernabe. *History of the Inca Empire.* Austin, TX: University of Texas Press, 1983.

Hemming, John. *The Conquest of the Incas.* New York: Harcourt Brace Jovanovich, 1970.

Malpass, Michael A. *Daily Life in the Inca Empire.* Westport, CT: Greenwood Press, 1996.

Marrin, Albert. *Inca & Spaniard: Pizarro and the Conquest of Peru.* New York: Atheneum, 1989.

Martell, Hazel Marry. *Civilizations of Peru Before 1535.* Austin, TX: Raintree Steck-Vaughn, 1999.

Prescott, William H. *History of the Conquest of Peru.* New York: The Modern Library, 1998.

INDEX

Index

About the Author

Fred Ramen is a writer and computer programmer who lives in New York City. His previous titles for the Rosen Publishing Group include biographies of Albert Speer and Joe Montana. Among his interests are military history, science fiction, and French cuisine.

Photo Credits

Cover © Réunion des Musées Nationaux/Art Resource, NY; pp. 4, 38–39, 40, 55, 101 © Culver Pictures, Inc.; pp. 8, 16 © Archivo Iconografico, S.A./Corbis; pp. 10–11, 13, 18–19, 23, 25, 28, 53, 62–63, 65, 73, 76–77, 88 © North Wind Picture Archives; pp. 21, 35 © Bettmann/Corbis; pp. 32–33 © Maps.com/Corbis; p. 43 © Jorge Provenza/Art Resource, NY; p. 46 © Kenneth Murray, Photo Researchers; p. 48 © Werner Forman/Art Resource, NY; p. 50 (left) © Bettmann/Corbis; p. 50 (right) © Gianni Dagli Orti/Corbis; pp. 58–89, 95 © Hulton/Archive/Getty Images; p. 68 © The Art Archive/Album/Joseph Martin; p. 70 © Michel Zabel/Art Resource, NY; p. 79 © The Art Archive/Bruning Museum Lambayeque Peru/Mireille Vautier; p. 81 © The Granger Collection; pp. 84–85 © Corbis; p. 86 © Victoria and Albert Museum/London/Art Resource, NY; p. 91 © The Art Archive/Museo Pedro de Osma Lima/Mireille Vautier; p. 93 © Allison Wright/Corbis; p. 100 © Vanni/Art Resource, NY.

Series Design and Layout

Tahara Hasan

Editor

Joann Jovinelly